Team Spirit

THE COLORADO ROCKIES

BY

MARK STEWART

Content Consultant
James L. Gates, Jr.
Library Director
National Baseball Hall of Fame and Museum

NORWOOD HOUSE PRESS
CHICAGO, ILLINOIS

Norwood House Press
P.O. Box 316598
Chicago, Illinois 60631

For information regarding Norwood House Press, please visit our website at:
www.norwoodhousepress.com or call 866-565-2900.

All photos courtesy of Getty Images except the following:
Topps, Inc. (14, 21 bottom, 40 top left);
Black Book archives (20).
Cover photo by Doug Pensinger/Getty Images.
Special thanks to Topps, Inc.

Editor: Mike Kennedy
Designer: Ron Jaffe
Project Management: Black Book Partners, LLC.
Special thanks to Hans Buenning, Roger Castle, and Diane Mayer.

Library of Congress Cataloging-in-Publication Data

Stewart, Mark, 1960-
  The Colorado Rockies / by Mark Stewart ; content consultant James L.
Gates.
      p. cm. -- (Team spirit)
  Summary: "Presents the history, accomplishments and key personalities of
the Colorado Rockies baseball team. Includes timelines, quotes, maps,
glossary and websites"--Provided by publisher.
  Includes bibliographical references and index.
  ISBN-13: 978-1-59953-166-3 (library edition : alk. paper)
  ISBN-10: 1-59953-166-6 (library edition : alk. paper)
  1. Colorado Rockies (Baseball team)--History--Juvenile literature. I.
Gates, James L. II. Title.
GV875.C78S837 2008
796.357'640978883--dc22
                                                            2007040056

Manufactured in the United States of America.

COVER PHOTO: The Rockies celebrate a win during the 2007 season.

Table of Contents

SPORTS WORDS & VOCABULARY WORDS: In this book, you will find many words that are new to you. You may also see familiar words used in new ways. The glossary on page 46 gives the meanings of baseball words, as well as "everyday" words that have special baseball meanings. These words appear in **bold type** throughout the book. The glossary on page 47 gives the meanings of vocabulary words that are not related to baseball. They appear in ***bold italic type*** throughout the book.

Meet the Rockies

Hit home runs and ask questions later. For many seasons, that was the *motto* of the Colorado Rockies. Their players strode confidently into the batter's box looking to hammer pitches over the fence. When you bought a ticket to a Rockies game, you could expect to see some great hitting.

The Rockies are still one of baseball's best-hitting teams. Over the years, however, they have gained skill and confidence in all *aspects* of baseball. Today, they are just as likely to hear cheers for a well-placed bunt, a great catch, a daring slide into home plate, or a beautifully pitched game.

This book tells the story of the Rockies. They run the bases hard and dive for balls on defense. They make good pitches when they need to and bring the fans to their feet with game-winning hits. In other words, they play exciting, *competitive*—Colorado Rockies—baseball.

The Rockies congratulate each other after a victory in 2007.

Way Back When

When sports fans in Denver, Colorado learned that they would be getting one of the two new teams in the **National League (NL)**, they were overjoyed. Baseball had been very popular in the state for a long time at every level—from Little League right up through the **minor leagues**. After many years of waiting for a team of its own in the **majors**, Denver was finally a big-league baseball town.

On April 9th, 1993, a record crowd of 80,277 fans filled the stands—the most ever for an Opening Day game. The Rockies sold 4,483,350 tickets that first season. That also set a new record. Colorado fans watched a club built around power hitters such as Andres Galarraga, Dante Bichette, Vinny Castilla, and Charlie Hayes.

The pitching was another matter. Colorado pitchers struggled when they took the mound at home. The Rockies played their games in Mile High Stadium, where the air was thinner and drier than in other ballparks. Many fly balls that would have been outs at a lower *altitude* hit the fence or flew over it. Naturally, Colorado's outfielders played extra-deep. But this meant that many

short fly balls fell in front of them for singles. Colorado's **pitching staff** *cringed* when any ball was hit to the outfield.

Of course, the Rockies' hitters loved to play at home. They hit for very high averages and slugged home runs at a record-breaking pace. Many players who wore a Colorado uniform for just a couple of seasons enjoyed the best years of their careers—including Ellis Burks, Juan Pierre, Jeffrey Hammonds, Preston Wilson, and Charles Johnson.

LEFT: Andres Galarraga bumps forearms with Dante Bichette.
ABOVE: Mile High Stadium, a ballpark that hitters loved.

Slowly but surely, the Rockies learned how to gain a home-field advantage. They had a winning record in just their third season and made it to the **playoffs** as the NL **Wild Card**. The stars of the 1995 team included Galarraga, Bichette, Castilla, Walt Weiss, and Larry Walker.

Walker would become one of the best players in baseball. He won three batting championships and five **Gold Gloves**, and was named the league's **Most Valuable Player (MVP)** in 1997.

That same year, Walker was joined in the **lineup** by a hot-hitting **rookie** named Todd Helton. The pair gave Colorado a great one-two punch for many seasons. Helton developed into a superstar **slugger** and a great fielder. He was the leader of the Rockies as they built a new team for the 21st *century*.

LEFT: Todd Helton, Colorado's most dangerous hitter for nearly 10 seasons.
ABOVE: Larry Walker, who teamed with Helton to give the Rockies a feared batting duo.

The Team Today

The Rockies are known for their excellent hitting. In recent years, they have developed many good pitchers, too. In 2002, the team helped its pitchers by building a humidor for storing its baseballs. The company that makes baseballs agreed that the dry air of Colorado was making the balls too light. The humidor keeps baseballs the exact same size and weight as when they leave the factory.

Colorado pitchers now throw with much more confidence. Players such as Aaron Cook, Jeff Francis, Brian Fuentes, and Manny Corpas have found great success pitching in their home park.

The Colorado hitters are happy, too. They may lose a few home runs, but that's okay. The Rockies are more concerned with hitting the ball hard. They don't try to slam every pitch out of the stadium. With Todd Helton leading the way for young stars such as Matt Holliday, Garrett Atkins, Brad Hawpe, and Troy Tulowitzki, the Rockies are ready to win the **World Series**.

Troy Tulowitzki and Matt Holliday celebrate a big win with a high five.

Home Turf

The Rockies spent their first two seasons in Mile High Stadium. It was also home to the Denver Broncos football team. Fans loved the Rockies and showed it by attending games in amazing numbers.

In 1995, the Rockies moved into Coors Field, which was built specifically for baseball. Fans love the stadium because it has an old-time feel to it but with all the modern conveniences. The food is very tasty, especially the famous foot-long hot dogs.

The **bleachers** in deep center field at the ballpark are known as the Rockpile. A solid line of purple seats stretches all the way around the stadium. Each of these seats measures exactly one mile above sea level.

BY THE NUMBERS

- *The stadium has 50,445 seats.*
- *The stadium cost $215 million to build.*
- *The distance from home plate to the left field foul pole is 347 feet.*
- *The distance from home plate to the center field fence is 415 feet.*
- *The distance from home plate to the right field foul pole is 350 feet.*

Fans who sit in the Rockpile at Colorado's stadium get a wonderful view of the field and downtown Denver.

Dressed for Success

Many teams have changed their uniform styles and colors since 1993, the year the Rockies joined the National League. The Rockies, meanwhile, have barely changed theirs at all. Colorado's combination of purple, black, and silver was very popular with baseball fans during that first season, and it remains a hit today. Colorado has always had a uniform with a pinstripe design, too. The Rockies have also worn sleeveless jerseys.

The team's **logo** also looks the same as it did in the early 1990s. It shows a baseball flying through the Rocky Mountains. Like Colorado's uniforms, the logo also uses purple. The team's cap features *CR* in bold letters. In some years, the *CR* has appeared on the players' stirrup socks, too.

Alex Cole models Colorado's uniform from the team's first season.

UNIFORM BASICS

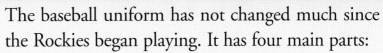

The baseball uniform has not changed much since the Rockies began playing. It has four main parts:

- a cap or batting helmet with a sun visor
- a top with a player's number on the back
- pants that reach down between the ankle and the knee
- stirrup-style socks

The uniform top sometimes has a player's name on the back. The team's name, city, or logo is usually on the front. Baseball teams wear light-colored uniforms when they play at home and darker styles when they play on the road.

For more than 100 years, baseball uniforms were made of wool *flannel* and were very baggy. This helped the sweat *evaporate* and gave players the freedom to move around. Today's uniforms are made of *synthetic* fabrics that stretch with players and keep them dry and cool.

Willy Taveras wears one of Colorado's 2007 road uniforms.

We Won!

When the Rockies joined the National League in 1993, their plan was to find powerful hitters who could take advantage of the dry, thin air in their stadium. Fans came out by the millions to watch the "Blake Street Bombers" slug home runs. Andres Galarraga, Vinny Castilla, Larry Walker, and Dante Bichette each hit more than 30 home runs in 1995. That season, the Rockies made it to the playoffs. This was quite a feat for a three-year-old team!

After 1995, the Rockies kept looking for hitters who would do well in Colorado. In the seasons that followed, Colorado scored a lot of runs, but the team failed to reach the playoffs again. In fact, most years the Rockies had a losing record.

The Rockies soon decided to rebuild their team with young players from within their organization. It took a few seasons, but by 2007, Colorado had an awesome

team. The Rockies fought hard all year long and tied for the NL Wild Card. They then beat the San Diego Padres in a one-game playoff to move on to the **Division Series** against the Philadelphia Phillies.

Jeff Francis pitched Colorado to a 4–2 victory in the opening game against the Phillies. One day later, Troy Tulowitzki and Matt Holliday hit home runs in the first inning, and Colorado went on to win Game Two by a score of 10–5. The Rockies took the third game 2–1 to sweep the series.

Next came the Arizona Diamondbacks in the **National League Championship Series (NLCS)**. The first team to win four games would be NL champions and go to the World Series. In Game One, Francis pitched well again, and the Rockies won 5–1. Game Two was an exciting contest that lasted 11 innings. Outfielder Willy Taveras saved Colorado with a diving catch in the seventh inning. Later, he pushed

LEFT: Jeff Francis winds up for a pitch during the 2007 playoffs.
ABOVE: Willy Taveras makes a diving catch in Game Two of the NLCS.

home the winning run when he drew a walk with the bases loaded.

The series moved from Arizona to Colorado for Game Three. With the home crowd cheering loudly, the Rockies won 4–1. The winning hit was a home run by Yorvit Torrealba in the sixth inning. The Colorado catcher was not known for his power hitting, but like many Rockies, he played his best when the team needed him most.

The Rockies' ballpark was rocking in Game Four. The team exploded for six runs in the fourth inning. Holliday hit a three-run home run to cap off the scoring. In the ninth inning, **relief pitcher** Manny Corpas slammed the door shut, and the Rockies were NL champions.

The Rockies were a hot team. Unfortunately, they met a club in the World Series that was playing even better. The Boston Red Sox swept Colorado in four games. Rockies fans were still happy. They knew they had been treated to a very special performance by a very special team.

LEFT: Yorvit Torrealba celebrates his home run against the Arizona Diamondbacks in Game Three.   **ABOVE**: The Rockies congratulate Matt Holliday after his homer in Game Four of the NLCS.

Go-To Guys

To be a true star in baseball, you need more than a quick bat and a strong arm. You have to be a "go-to guy"—someone the manager wants on the pitcher's mound or in the batter's box when it matters most. Fans of the Rockies have had a lot to cheer about over the years, including these great stars …

THE PIONEERS

ANDRES GALARRAGA   First Baseman

• BORN: 6/18/1961   • PLAYED FOR TEAM: 1993 TO 1997

Andres Galarraga was known as the "Big Cat" for his quickness and grace in the field. However, it was his hitting that made him a favorite of Colorado fans. In his first year with the team, he won the NL batting championship with a .370 average.

DANTE BICHETTE   Outfielder

• BORN: 11/18/1963   • PLAYED FOR TEAM: 1993 TO 1999

Dante Bichette hit for a good average and had excellent power. He was also one of the team's best baserunners. In 1995, Bichette just missed winning the NL **Triple Crown** with a .340 batting average, 40 home runs, and 128 **runs batted in (RBI)**.

ABOVE: Andres Galarraga
TOP RIGHT: Vinny Castilla   **BOTTOM RIGHT**: Larry Walker

20

VINNY CASTILLA — Third Baseman

- BORN: 7/4/1967
- PLAYED FOR TEAM: 1993 TO 1999, 2004 & 2006

Vinny Castilla was one of Colorado's most popular players. He hit 40 or more home runs three years in a row for the Rockies during the 1990s. In 2004, Castilla returned to the club after four years away and led the NL with 131 runs batted in.

ELLIS BURKS — Outfielder

- BORN: 9/11/1964
- PLAYED FOR TEAM: 1994 TO 1998

Ellis Burks was a great hitter who had the best season of his career with the Rockies in 1996. That year, he hit .344 with 45 doubles, 40 home runs, and 128 runs batted in. He also scored 142 runs and stole 32 bases.

LARRY WALKER — Outfielder

- BORN: 12/1/1966
- PLAYED FOR TEAM: 1995 TO 2004

Larry Walker was the best **all-around** player the Rockies ever had. He was an amazing hitter, excellent fielder, and a smart baserunner. In 1997, Walker hit .366 with 49 homers and 33 stolen bases. He was named NL MVP that year.

LARRY WALKER

TODD HELTON   **First Baseman**

- BORN: 8/20/1973
- FIRST YEAR WITH TEAM: 1997

Todd Helton took over first base from Andres Galarraga and won three Gold Glove awards. He also led the NL in batting in 2000. Helton was known as one of the sport's nice guys and made friends all over baseball.

GARRETT ATKINS   **Third Baseman**

- BORN: 12/12/1979   • FIRST YEAR WITH TEAM: 2003

Garrett Atkins was one of the best college hitters in the nation when the Rockies **drafted** him in 2000. He continued to swing the bat well for Colorado and was the first rookie ever to lead the team in runs batted in.

MATT HOLLIDAY   **Outfielder**

- BORN: 1/15/1980
- FIRST YEAR WITH TEAM: 2004

Matt Holliday was a great football player in high school, but he decided that baseball was his best sport. Colorado fans were thrilled with his choice. In 2007, Holliday batted .340 with 36 home runs and 137 runs batted in, and led the Rockies to the NL pennant.

ABOVE: Matt Holliday and Garrett Atkins
TOP RIGHT: Brad Hawpe   **BOTTOM RIGHT**: Troy Tulowitzki

BRAD HAWPE — Outfielder

- BORN: 6/22/1979
- FIRST YEAR WITH TEAM: 2004

The Rockies drafted Brad Hawpe because they wanted a winner. He led his teams to championships in high school and college, and he had a reputation for doing his best under pressure. Soon after arriving in Colorado, Hawpe brought fans to their feet with his long home runs.

JEFF FRANCIS — Pitcher

- BORN: 1/8/1981 • FIRST YEAR WITH TEAM: 2004

The Rockies drafted Jeff Francis hoping he might become the team's ace pitcher some day. He was named Colorado's best player in the minor leagues in 2004. By 2006, he had won more games than any left-hander in team history.

TROY TULOWITZKI — Shortstop

- BORN: 10/10/1984
- FIRST YEAR WITH TEAM: 2006

The Rockies picked Troy Tulowitzki in the first round of the 2005 draft. They liked his size, speed, and strength. In 2007, Tulowitzki hit more than 20 home runs and made an *unassisted* triple play.

On the Sidelines

Colorado's first manager was Don Baylor. He was known for his great skill and *patience* as a player and then as a batting coach. With Baylor in the dugout, the Rockies won 440 games from 1993 to 1998. That made Colorado one of the most successful **expansion teams** ever.

Jim Leyland managed the Rockies in 1999. Two years earlier, he had led the Florida Marlins to victory in the World Series. The Rockies were hoping he could do the same for them, but he retired after one season.

Clint Hurdle was named Colorado's manager in 2002. He was hired to mold the team's young players into stars. Hurdle knew all about this process. In the 1970s, he had been a young prospect with a bright future. He eventually learned that *potential* means nothing without hard work and constant improvement. Hurdle helped players such as Jeff Francis, Garrett Atkins, Troy Tulowitzki, Brad Hawpe, and Matt Holliday become stars.

Clint Hurdle congratulates Seth Smith during the 2007 playoffs. Hurdle led the Rockies to their first NL pennant that season.

One Great Day

The Rockies were the hottest team in baseball during the final month of the 2007 season. They won 14 of their final 15 games to finish with 89 victories—just enough to tie the San Diego Padres for the NL Wild Card. An extra game was scheduled to decide who would move forward and who would go home.

More than 48,000 fans jammed into Coors Field to cheer for the Rockies. They saw one of the greatest games in history. Yorvit Torrealba and Todd Helton launched home runs to give Colorado the lead. Adrian Gonzalez belted a **grand slam** to bring the Padres back. In the seventh inning, Garrett Atkins hit a ball that looked like a home run, but the umpires ruled that it had not cleared the fence. They made Atkins stop at second base. Instead of leading the game 7–5, the Rockies were only ahead by one run, 6–5. The Padres scored in the eighth inning to tie the game.

The two teams battled into **extra innings**. In the top of the 13th, the Padres went ahead 8–6. Down to their last three outs, the Rockies faced Trevor Hoffman. He had **saved** more games than any pitcher in history.

The Rockies go wild after their incredible win over the San Diego Padres.

The fans jumped to their feet when Kaz Matsui lined a double off Hoffman. Troy Tulowitzki followed with a double of his own to drive in Matsui. Next up was Matt Holliday, who legged out a triple that tied the score at 8–8.

Jamey Carroll then hit a fly ball to right field. Holliday tagged up and raced toward home. He slid headfirst and touched home plate an instant before he was tagged by catcher Michael Barrett. The umpire saw this and gave the safe sign. The Rockies were Wild Card champions. They won 9–8 on one of the most exciting plays anyone could remember!

Legend Has It

Which Colorado player once lost his job to football star Peyton Manning?

LEGEND HAS IT that Todd Helton did. Helton was the starting quarterback at the University of Tennessee in 1994. He injured his knee in a game and was replaced by Manning, who was a freshman at the time. By the time Helton's knee healed, it was too late—Manning was "the man" at Tennessee.

Who was the Rockies' best home-field hitter?

LEGEND HAS IT that Larry Walker was. Coors Field is known as a great hitter's park. The ball carries very well when it soars high in the air. There is a lot of room in the outfield for hits to drop in. Many Colorado hitters bat over .300 at home. In 1999, Walker did even better than that. He hit a whopping .461 at home.

What was the best day for Rockies' hitters in team history?

LEGEND HAS IT that it was a 13–6 victory in 1999. The Rockies have played a lot of high-scoring games in their history, but no contest was more memorable than the one against the Chicago Cubs on May 5th of that year. Colorado scored in the first inning and then **plated** at least one run in every inning after. In the process, the Rockies became just the third team in the 20th century to score a run in every inning of a nine-inning game.

LEFT: Todd Helton throws a pass for the University of Tennessee.
ABOVE: Larry Walker waits for a pitch.

It Really Happened

hortstops are always thinking. When a ball is hit to them, they must know exactly what to do with it. There is no time for *hesitation*. In the seventh inning of a 2007 game against the Atlanta Braves, Troy Tulowitzki was thinking about the two runners on base and the batter standing at home plate.

The game was tied. Kelly Johnson was leading off second base and Edgar Renteria was leading off first. There were no outs and Chipper Jones was at bat. The count reached three balls and two strikes. The runners took off on the next pitch, and Jones slammed a line drive up the middle.

Tulowitzki darted to his left and snared the ball in the web of his mitt for one out. He cut toward second base and stepped on it before Johnson could get back there. That made two outs. Tulowitzki looked up to see Renteria, who was caught far off first base. The young shortstop tagged him for the third out. It was just the 13th unassisted triple play in history.

"It kind of just fell into my lap, but I'll take it," Tulowitzki said after the game.

Troy Tulowitzki tags Edgar Renteria for the third out of his
unassisted triple play.

Matt Holliday, the left fielder, told reporters that he had been
thinking about a triple play an instant before Jones hit the ball.

"Not that I predicted it or anything," he said, "I was just
thinking that, so it was kind of weird. I watched it unfold right
before my eyes."

Team Spirit

There are no fans quite like Colorado baseball fans. They will put up with blazing heat, bone-chilling snow, and low temperatures. They proved this in the team's first season, when more than four million fans bought tickets to see the Rockies play. Never before—in any sport—had the people of a community welcomed their team so *enthusiastically*.

Baseball was hardly new to the city of Denver. Minor-league teams called the city home for more than a century. Some *superb* players wore the uniform of the Denver Bears on their way to the majors, including Tim Raines and Graig Nettles.

Today, the Rockies draw fans from all over the region. They come from Kansas, Nebraska, Wyoming, and New Mexico to watch the team play. They also come to Colorado to enjoy other outdoor sports. The Rockies play in one of the only cities in America where you can ski in the morning and watch a ballgame in the evening.

The Colorado fans cheer on the Rockies. Their support helped the team win the NL pennant in 2007.

Timeline

Ellis
Burks

1993
The Rockies go
67–95 in their
first season.

1996
Ellis Burks leads
the NL in **total bases**.

1995
The Rockies win
the NL Wild Card.

1997
Larry Walker wins
the NL MVP award.

1998
The **All-Star Game** is
played at Coors Field.

Walt Weiss,
the shortstop on
the 1995 Rockies.

NFL star John Elway
takes a swing during a
1998 All-Star Game
celebrity contest.

Larry
Walker

Matt
Holliday

2002
Larry Walker
wins his fifth
Gold Glove for
the Rockies.

2005
Matt Holliday ties a team record
with eight runs batted in in a game.

2000
Todd Helton
wins the NL
batting title.

2001
The Rockies draw more
than three million fans for
the ninth year in a row.

2007
The Rockies reach the
NLCS for the first time.

Todd
Helton

Helton and Manny
Corpas celebrate
a playoff victory
in 2007.

Fun Facts

PINCH ME, I'M DREAMING

John Vander Wal had a dream season for the Rockies in 1995. He came off the bench to set a record with 28 **pinch hits** that year.

POWER & SPEED

The Rockies were very busy in 1996. That season they became the first team to hit 200 home runs and steal 200 bases in the same year.

BIG BLAST FOR THE BIG CAT

Andres Galarraga hit one of the longest home runs in history against the Florida Marlins in 1997. Some believe it traveled more than 520 feet.

ABOVE: John Vander Wal
TOP RIGHT: Matt Holliday bats against his brother.
BOTTOM RIGHT: Ellis Burks

PUT ONE OVER, BRO

When Matt Holliday competed in the Home Run Derby at the 2007 All-Star Game, he got to choose his own pitcher. He selected his brother, Josh.

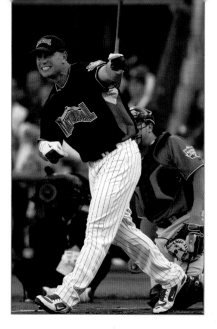

I OWE YOU ONE

When Todd Helton won the batting championship in 2000, he did it with a borrowed bat. Early in the year, he had grabbed one that belonged to his teammate, Jeff Manto. He liked it so much that he used Manto's bats the rest of the season.

FAST COMPANY

In 1996, Ellis Burks became only the second player ever to get 200 hits, 40 home runs, and 30 stolen bases in the same season. The first was **Hall of Famer** Henry Aaron.

Talking Baseball

"There are a lot of guys I can learn from in this locker room, but if I have to say something, I will say it."

—Troy Tulowitzki, on being
a young leader

"I thrive on the electricity I get from the fans. The heat, the sweat, and emotions— I like it when they get involved."

—Andres Galarraga, on playing
in front of huge crowds
in Colorado

"I want people to expect more from me because I expect more. If you don't set goals high, you're not trying."

—Todd Helton, on reaching
your goals

"I like to be fair with the players, but there's a time for **discipline**."

> —*Don Baylor, on why managers have to be strict with their players*

"You have to look past the cool things and play the game. That's why you're here, to play the game."

> —*Matt Holliday, on the importance of learning the basics of baseball*

"It's definitely **satisfying** to be out there at the end of the game shaking hands with the guys."

> —*Jeff Francis, on pitching complete games*

"Whatever it takes to get a win, you should be out trying to do it."

> —*Larry Walker, on always looking for an edge in baseball*

LEFT: Troy Tulowitzki
ABOVE: Jeff Francis

For the Record

The great Rockies teams and players have left their marks on the record books. These are the "best of the best" …

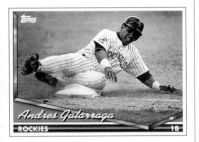

ROCKIES AWARD WINNERS

WINNER	AWARD	YEAR
Andres Galarraga	Comeback Player of the Year	1993
Don Baylor	Manager of the Year	1995
Larry Walker	Most Valuable Player	1997
Jason Jennings	Rookie of the Year*	2002
Matt Holliday	NLCS MVP	2007

The annual award given to each league's best first-year player.

ABOVE: Andres Galarraga   **BELOW**: Jason Jennings

ROCKIES ACHIEVEMENTS

ACHIEVEMENT	YEAR
NL Wild Card	1995
NL Wild Card	2007
NL Pennant Winners	2007

TOP LEFT: Jeff Francis fires a pitch during the 2007 season. **BOTTOM LEFT**: Clint Hurdle and Troy Tulowitzki shake hands after a win. **ABOVE**: Brad Hawpe, another star on the pennant winners.

41

Pinpoints

The history of a baseball team is made up of many smaller stories. These stories take place all over the map—not just in the city a team calls "home." Match the pushpins on these maps to the Team Facts and you will begin to see the story of the Rockies unfold!

TEAM FACTS

1 Denver, Colorado—*The Rockies have played here since 1993.*

2 West Palm Beach, Florida—*Dante Bichette was born here.*

3 Stillwater, Oklahoma—*Matt Holliday was born here.*

4 Knoxville, Tennessee—*Todd Helton was born here.*

5 Fort Campbell, Kentucky—*Aaron Cook was born here.*

6 Santa Clara, California—*Troy Tulowitzki was born here.*

7 Grand Rapids, Michigan—*John Vander Wal was born here.*

8 Tuxedo, New York—*Walt Weiss was born here.*

9 Osaka, Japan—*Kaz Matsui was born here.*

10 Caracas, Venezuela—*Andres Galarraga was born here.*

11 Oaxaca, Mexico—*Vinny Castilla was born here.*

12 Maple Ridge, British Columbia, Canada—*Larry Walker was born here.*

Aaron Cook

Play Ball

Baseball is a game played between two teams over nine innings. Teams take one turn at bat and one turn in the field during each inning. A turn at bat ends when three outs are made. The batters on the hitting team try to reach base safely. The players on the fielding team try to prevent this from happening.

In baseball, the ball is controlled by the pitcher. The pitcher must throw the ball to the batter, who decides whether or not to swing at each pitch. If a batter swings and misses, it is a strike. If the batter lets a good pitch go by, it is also a strike. If the batter swings and the ball does not stay in fair territory (between the v-shaped lines that begin at home plate) it is called "foul," and is counted as a strike. If the pitcher throws three strikes, the batter is out. If the pitcher throws four bad pitches before that, the batter is awarded first base. This is called a base-on-balls, or "walk."

When the batter swings the bat and hits the ball, everyone springs into action. If a fielder catches a batted ball before it hits the ground, the batter is out. If a fielder scoops the ball off the ground and throws it to first base before the batter arrives, the batter is out. If the batter reaches first base safely, he is credited with a hit. A one-base hit is called a single, a two-base hit is called a double, a three-base hit is called a triple, and a four-base hit is called a home run.

Runners who reach base are only safe when they are touching one of the bases. If they are caught between the bases, the fielders can tag them with the ball and record an out.

A batter who is able to circle the bases and make it back to home plate before three outs are made is credited with a run scored. The team with the most runs after nine innings is the winner.

Anyone who has played baseball (or softball) knows that it can be a complicated game. Every player on the field has a job to do. Different players have different strengths and weaknesses. The pitchers, batters, and managers make hundreds of decisions every game. The more you play and watch baseball, the more "little things" you are likely to notice. The next time you are at a game, look for these plays:

PLAY LIST

DOUBLE PLAY—A play where the fielding team is able to make two outs on one batted ball. This usually happens when a runner is on first base, and the batter hits a ground ball to one of the infielders. The base runner is forced out at second base and the ball is then thrown to first base before the batter arrives.

HIT AND RUN—A play where the runner on first base sprints to second base while the pitcher is throwing the ball to the batter. When the second baseman or shortstop moves toward the base to wait for the catcher's throw, the batter tries to hit the ball to the place that the fielder has just left. If the batter swings and misses, the fielding team can tag the runner out.

INTENTIONAL WALK—A play when the pitcher throws four bad pitches on purpose, allowing the batter to walk to first base. This happens when the pitcher would much rather face the next batter—and is willing to risk putting a runner on base.

SACRIFICE BUNT—A play where the batter makes an out on purpose so that a teammate can move to the next base. On a bunt, the batter tries to "deaden" the pitch with the bat instead of swinging at it.

SHOESTRING CATCH—A play where an outfielder catches a short hit an inch or two above the ground, near the tops of his shoes. It is not easy to run as fast as you can and lower your glove without slowing down. It can be risky, too. If a fielder misses a shoestring catch, the ball might roll all the way to the fence.

Glossary

BASEBALL WORDS TO KNOW

ALL-AROUND—Good at all parts of the game.

ALL-STAR GAME—Baseball's annual game featuring the best players from the American League and National League.

BLEACHERS—The unprotected seats located in the outfield, where fans get "bleached" by the sun.

DIVISION SERIES—A series played to determine which teams have a chance to advance to the World Series.

DRAFTED—Selected at the annual meeting at which teams take turns choosing the best players in high school and college.

EXPANSION TEAMS—New teams added to a league.

EXTRA INNINGS—Innings played when a game is tied after nine innings.

GOLD GLOVES—Awards given each year to baseball's best fielders.

GRAND SLAM—A home run with the bases loaded.

HALL OF FAMER—A player honored by baseball's Hall of Fame, a museum in Cooperstown, New York.

LINEUP—The list of players who are playing in a game.

MAJORS—The top level of professional baseball leagues. The American League and National League make up today's major leagues. Sometimes called the "big leagues."

MINOR LEAGUES—The many professional leagues that help develop players for the major leagues.

MOST VALUABLE PLAYER (MVP)—An award given each year to each league's top player; an MVP is also selected for the World Series and All-Star Game.

NATIONAL LEAGUE (NL)—The older of the two major leagues; the NL began play in 1876 and the American League started in 1901.

NATIONAL LEAGUE CHAMPIONSHIP SERIES (NLCS)—The competition that has decided the National League pennant since 1969.

PINCH HITS—Hits made by a batter taking a teammate's turn to bat.

PITCHING STAFF—The group of players who pitch for a team.

PLATED—Scored or drove home a runner.

PLAYOFFS—The games played after the regular season to determine which teams will advance to the World Series.

PROSPECT—A player who is expected to become a star.

RELIEF PITCHER—A pitcher who is brought into a game to replace another pitcher. Relief pitchers can be seen warming up in the bullpen.

ROOKIE—A player in his first season.

RUNS BATTED IN (RBI)—A statistic that counts the number of runners a batter drives home.

SAVED—Recorded the last out in a team's win. A pitcher on the mound for the last out of a close victory is credited with a "save."

SLUGGER—A powerful hitter.

TOTAL BASES—A player's total number of bases when you add up all of his hits.

TRIPLE CROWN—An honor given to a player who leads the league in home runs, batting average, and runs batted in.

WILD CARD—A playoff spot reserved for the team with the best record that has not won its division.

WORLD SERIES—The world championship series played between the winners of the National League and American League.

OTHER WORDS TO KNOW

ALTITUDE—The height of something above sea level.

ASPECTS—Areas of concentration.

CENTURY—A period of 100 years.

COMPETITIVE—Having a strong desire to win.

CRINGED—Drew back in fear.

DISCIPLINE—Behavior that follows rules.

ENTHUSIASTICALLY—Filled with strong excitement.

EVAPORATE—Disappear, or turn into vapor.

FLANNEL—A soft wool or cotton material.

HESITATION—A pause.

LOGO—A symbol or design that represents a company or team.

MOTTO—A short expression used again and again.

PATIENCE—The ability to wait calmly.

POTENTIAL—The ability to become better.

SATISFYING—Having a feeling of happiness.

SUPERB—Of the highest quality.

SYNTHETIC—Made in a laboratory, not in nature.

UNASSISTED—Without help from anyone.

Places to Go

ON THE ROAD

COLORADO ROCKIES
2001 Blake Street
Denver, Colorado   80205
(303) 312-2110

**NATIONAL BASEBALL
HALL OF FAME AND MUSEUM**
25 Main Street
Cooperstown, New York 13326
(888) 425-5633
www.baseballhalloffame.org

ON THE WEB

THE COLORADO ROCKIES   www.coloradorockies.com
  • *Learn more about the Rockies*

MAJOR LEAGUE BASEBALL   www.mlb.com
  • *Learn more about all the major league teams*

MINOR LEAGUE BASEBALL   www.minorleaguebaseball.com
  • *Learn more about the minor leagues*

ON THE BOOKSHELF

To learn more about the sport of baseball, look for these books at your library or bookstore:

  • Kelly, James. *Baseball*. New York, New York: DK, 2005.

  • Jacobs, Greg. *The Everything Kids' Baseball Book*. Cincinnati, Ohio: Adams Media Corporation, 2006.

  • Stewart, Mark and Kennedy, Mike. *Long Ball: The Legend and Lore of the Home Run.* Minneapolis, Minnesota: Millbrook Press, 2006.

Index

PAGE NUMBERS IN **BOLD** REFER TO ILLUSTRATIONS.

The Team

MARK STEWART has written more than 25 books on baseball, and over 100 sports books for kids. He grew up in New York City during the 1960s rooting for the Yankees and Mets, and now takes his two daughters, Mariah and Rachel, to the same ball-parks. Mark comes from a family of writers. His grand-father was Sunday Editor of the *New York Times* and his mother was Articles Editor of *Ladies' Home Journal* and *McCall's*. Mark has profiled hundreds of athletes over the last 20 years. He has also written several books about his native New York and New Jersey, his home today. Mark is a graduate of Duke University, with a degree in history. He lives with his daughters and wife, Sarah, overlooking Sandy Hook, NJ.

JAMES L. GATES, JR. has served as Library Director at the National Baseball Hall of Fame since 1995. He had previously served in academic libraries for almost fifteen years. He holds degrees from Belmont Abbey College, the University of Notre Dame, and Indiana University. During his career Jim has authored several academic articles and has served in an editorial capacity on multiple book, magazine, and museum publications, and he also serves as host for the Annual Cooperstown Symposium on Baseball and American Culture. He is an ardent Baltimore Orioles fan and enjoys watching baseball with his wife and two children.